SOMEWHERE BETWEEN THE START OF THE TRAIL
AND THE END IS THE MYSTERY
WHY WE CHOOSE TO WALK.

UNKNOWN ·

IF FOUND, PLEASE CONTACT

_____

PHILINE THÖLE, BERLIN 2022

INFO@WANDERLUSTNOMADE.COM
WWW.WANDERLUSTNOMADE.COM

INDEPENDENTLY PUBLISHED

HIKING - ROUTE

_____

_____

START | LOCATION | DATE

END | LOCATION | DATE

IF YOU DON'T KNOW WHERE YOU WANT TO GO,
DON'T BE SURPRISED IF YOU END UP
SOMEWHERE COMPLETELY DIFFERENT.

MARK TWAIN

MY EXPECTATIONS

MY REASONS FOR HIKING

- ◯ ADVENTURE
- ◯ CULTURE
- ◯ HISTORY
- ◯ LANDSCAPE
- ◯ SPORT

- ◯ SELF-DISCOVERY
- ◯ SLOWING DOWN
- ◯ LONGING FOR SIMPLICITY
- ◯ I HAVE TO COME ALONG
- ◯ _____

- ◯ THIS IS MY FIRST HIKE
- ◯ I'M READY FOR ANOTHER GO
- ◯ I AM INFESTED WITH THE HIKING-VIRUS

HOW I HIKE THE TRAIL

- ◯ ALONE
- ◯ WITH _____
- ◯ AS A GROUP (LEADED) _____

HIKING SPEED

◯ SNAIL ◯ TORTOISE ◯ LEMMING ◯ BEAR ◯ HARE

WHERE I WILL SLEEP

- ◯ COWBOY CAMPING
- ◯ TARP ETC.
- ◯ TENT/HAMMOCK/ETC.
- ◯ CAMPSITE
- ◯ SHELTER
- ◯ HUT/BOTHY

- ◯ HOSTEL
- ◯ HOTEL
- ◯ FRIENDS
- ◯ TRAIL - ANGELS
- ◯ STRANGERS
- ◯ _____

WHAT AM I LOOKING FORWARD TO THE MOST?

WHY THIS ROUTE?

WHAT DO I WANT TO LEAVE BEHIND?

WHAT WILL PROBABLY BE DIFFICULT FOR ME?

OTHER ...

"TRAVELING - IT LEAVES YOU SPEECHLESS,
THEN TURNS YOU INTO A STORYTELLER."

IBN BATTUTA

ULTREIA!

GEARLIST

_____	☐	_____	☐
_____	☐	_____	☐
_____	☐	_____	☐
_____	☐	_____	☐
_____	☐	_____	☐
_____	☐	_____	☐
_____	☐	_____	☐
_____	☐	_____	☐
_____	☐	_____	☐
_____	☐	_____	☐
_____	☐	_____	☐
_____	☐	_____	☐
_____	☐	_____	☐
_____	☐	_____	☐
_____	☐	_____	☐
_____	☐	_____	☐
_____	☐	_____	☐

NEW GEAR IDEAS FOR NEXT TIME

BASE-WEIGHT _____   START-WEIGHT _____

STAGE

START LOCATION

DESTINATION

DATE

START TIME

DISTANCE

ARRIVAL TIME

ACCOMMODATION

MOOD

EFFORT

FLUID INTAKE

FOOT-HEALTH

BACKPACK-WEIGHT

STAGE - ATTRACTIVENESS

I WILL REMEMBER THE DAY FOR . . .

TODAY'S SUCSESS

WEATHER AND TEMPERATURE

WISH FOR TOMORROW

TODAY I'M GRATEFUL FOR . . .

DISTANCE SO FAR

STILL TO GO

ROOM FOR THOUGHTS, SKETCHES, PICTURES OR NOTES

STAGE

START LOCATION

DESTINATION

DATE

START TIME

DISTANCE

ARRIVAL TIME

ACCOMMODATION

MOOD

EFFORT

FLUID INTAKE

FOOT-HEALTH

BACKPACK-WEIGHT

STAGE - ATTRACTIVENESS

I WILL REMEMBER THE DAY FOR . . .

TODAY'S SUCSESS

WEATHER AND TEMPERATURE

WISH FOR TOMORROW

TODAY I'M GRATEFUL FOR . . .

DISTANCE SO FAR

STILL TO GO

ROOM FOR THOUGHTS, SKETCHES, PICTURES OR NOTES

STAGE

START LOCATION

DESTINATION

DATE

START TIME

DISTANCE

ARRIVAL TIME

ACCOMMODATION

I WILL REMEMBER THE DAY FOR . . .

MOOD

EFFORT

FLUID INTAKE

FOOT-HEALTH

BACKPACK-WEIGHT

STAGE - ATTRACTIVENESS

TODAY'S SUCSESS

WEATHER AND TEMPERATURE

WISH FOR TOMORROW

TODAY I'M GRATEFUL FOR . . .

DISTANCE SO FAR

STILL TO GO

ROOM FOR THOUGHTS, SKETCHES, PICTURES OR NOTES

STAGE

START LOCATION

DESTINATION

DATE

START TIME

DISTANCE

ARRIVAL TIME

ACCOMMODATION

I WILL REMEMBER THE DAY FOR . . .

MOOD

EFFORT

FLUID INTAKE

FOOT-HEALTH

BACKPACK-WEIGHT

STAGE - ATTRACTIVENESS

TODAY'S SUCSESS

WEATHER AND TEMPERATURE

WISH FOR TOMORROW

TODAY I'M GRATEFUL FOR . . .

DISTANCE SO FAR

STILL TO GO

ROOM FOR THOUGHTS, SKETCHES, PICTURES OR NOTES

STAGE

START LOCATION

DESTINATION

DATE

START TIME

DISTANCE

ARRIVAL TIME

ACCOMMODATION

I WILL REMEMBER THE DAY FOR . . .

MOOD

EFFORT

FLUID INTAKE

FOOT-HEALTH

BACKPACK-WEIGHT

STAGE - ATTRACTIVENESS

TODAY'S SUCSESS

WEATHER AND TEMPERATURE

WISH FOR TOMORROW

TODAY I'M GRATEFUL FOR . . .

DISTANCE SO FAR

STILL TO GO

ROOM FOR THOUGHTS, SKETCHES, PICTURES OR NOTES

STAGE

START LOCATION

DESTINATION

DATE

START TIME

DISTANCE

ARRIVAL TIME

ACCOMMODATION

MOOD

EFFORT

FLUID INTAKE

FOOT-HEALTH

BACKPACK-WEIGHT

STAGE - ATTRACTIVENESS

I WILL REMEMBER THE DAY FOR . . .

TODAY'S SUCSESS

WEATHER AND TEMPERATURE

WISH FOR TOMORROW

TODAY I'M GRATEFUL FOR . . .

DISTANCE SO FAR

STILL TO GO

ROOM FOR THOUGHTS, SKETCHES, PICTURES OR NOTES

STAGE

START LOCATION

DESTINATION

DATE

START TIME

DISTANCE

ARRIVAL TIME

ACCOMMODATION

MOOD

EFFORT

FLUID INTAKE

FOOT-HEALTH

BACKPACK-WEIGHT

STAGE - ATTRACTIVENESS

I WILL REMEMBER THE DAY FOR . . .

TODAY'S SUCSESS

WEATHER AND TEMPERATURE

WISH FOR TOMORROW

TODAY I'M GRATEFUL FOR . . .

DISTANCE SO FAR

STILL TO GO

ROOM FOR THOUGHTS, SKETCHES, PICTURES OR NOTES

STAGE

START LOCATION

DESTINATION

DATE

START TIME

DISTANCE

ARRIVAL TIME

ACCOMMODATION

MOOD

EFFORT

FLUID INTAKE

FOOT-HEALTH

BACKPACK-WEIGHT

STAGE - ATTRACTIVENESS

I WILL REMEMBER THE DAY FOR . . .

TODAY'S SUCSESS

WEATHER AND TEMPERATURE

WISH FOR TOMORROW

TODAY I'M GRATEFUL FOR . . .

DISTANCE SO FAR

STILL TO GO

ROOM FOR THOUGHTS, SKETCHES, PICTURES OR NOTES

STAGE

START LOCATION

DESTINATION

DATE

START TIME

DISTANCE

ARRIVAL TIME

ACCOMMODATION

MOOD

EFFORT

FLUID INTAKE

I WILL REMEMBER THE DAY FOR . . .

FOOT-HEALTH

BACKPACK-WEIGHT

STAGE - ATTRACTIVENESS

TODAY'S SUCSESS

WEATHER AND TEMPERATURE

WISH FOR TOMORROW

TODAY I'M GRATEFUL FOR . . .

DISTANCE SO FAR

STILL TO GO

ROOM FOR THOUGHTS, SKETCHES, PICTURES OR NOTES

STAGE

START LOCATION

DESTINATION

DATE

START TIME

DISTANCE

ARRIVAL TIME

ACCOMMODATION

MOOD

EFFORT

FLUID INTAKE

FOOT-HEALTH

BACKPACK-WEIGHT

STAGE - ATTRACTIVENESS

I WILL REMEMBER THE DAY FOR . . .

TODAY'S SUCSESS

WEATHER AND TEMPERATURE

WISH FOR TOMORROW

TODAY I'M GRATEFUL FOR . . .

DISTANCE SO FAR

STILL TO GO

ROOM FOR THOUGHTS, SKETCHES, PICTURES OR NOTES

STAGE

START LOCATION

DESTINATION

DATE

START TIME

DISTANCE

ARRIVAL TIME

ACCOMMODATION ☺ ☺ ☹

I WILL REMEMBER THE DAY FOR . . .

MOOD
☺ ☺ ☺ ☹ ☹

EFFORT
◊ ◊ ◊ ◊ ◊

FLUID INTAKE
☺ ☺ ☺ ☹ ☹

FOOT-HEALTH
☺ ☺ ☺ ☹ ☹

BACKPACK-WEIGHT
☺ ☺ ☺ ☹ ☹

STAGE - ATTRACTIVENESS
♡ ♡ ♡ ♡ ♡

TODAY'S SUCSESS

WEATHER AND TEMPERATURE

WISH FOR TOMORROW

TODAY I'M GRATEFUL FOR . . .

DISTANCE SO FAR

STILL TO GO

ROOM FOR THOUGHTS, SKETCHES, PICTURES OR NOTES

STAGE

START LOCATION

DESTINATION

DATE

START TIME

DISTANCE

ARRIVAL TIME

ACCOMMODATION

MOOD

EFFORT

FLUID INTAKE

FOOT-HEALTH

BACKPACK-WEIGHT

STAGE - ATTRACTIVENESS

I WILL REMEMBER THE DAY FOR . . .

TODAY'S SUCSESS

WEATHER AND TEMPERATURE

WISH FOR TOMORROW

TODAY I'M GRATEFUL FOR . . .

DISTANCE SO FAR

STILL TO GO

ROOM FOR THOUGHTS, SKETCHES, PICTURES OR NOTES

STAGE

START LOCATION

DESTINATION

DATE

START TIME

DISTANCE

ARRIVAL TIME

ACCOMMODATION

MOOD

EFFORT

FLUID INTAKE

FOOT-HEALTH

BACKPACK-WEIGHT

STAGE - ATTRACTIVENESS

I WILL REMEMBER THE DAY FOR . . .

TODAY'S SUCSESS

WEATHER AND TEMPERATURE

WISH FOR TOMORROW

TODAY I'M GRATEFUL FOR . . .

DISTANCE SO FAR

STILL TO GO

ROOM FOR THOUGHTS, SKETCHES, PICTURES OR NOTES

STAGE

START LOCATION

DESTINATION

DATE

START TIME

DISTANCE

ARRIVAL TIME

ACCOMMODATION 😊 😐 ☹️

I WILL REMEMBER THE DAY FOR . . .

MOOD
😄 🙂 😐 🙁 😣

EFFORT
💧 💧 💧 💧 💧

FLUID INTAKE
😄 🙂 😐 🙁 😵

FOOT-HEALTH
😄 🙂 😐 😲 😵

BACKPACK-WEIGHT
😄 🙂 😐 🙁 😵

STAGE - ATTRACTIVENESS
♡ ♡ ♡ ♡ ♡

TODAY'S SUCSESS

WEATHER AND TEMPERATURE

WISH FOR TOMORROW

TODAY I'M GRATEFUL FOR . . .

DISTANCE SO FAR

STILL TO GO

ROOM FOR THOUGHTS, SKETCHES, PICTURES OR NOTES

STAGE

START LOCATION

DESTINATION

DATE

START TIME

DISTANCE

ARRIVAL TIME

ACCOMMODATION

MOOD

☺ ☺ ☺ ☹ ☹

EFFORT

◊ ◊ ◊ ◊ ◊

FLUID INTAKE

☺ ☺ ☺ ☹ ☹

I WILL REMEMBER THE DAY FOR . . .

FOOT-HEALTH

☺ ☺ ☺ ☺ ☹

BACKPACK-WEIGHT

☺ ☺ ☺ ☹ ☹

STAGE - ATTRACTIVENESS

♡ ♡ ♡ ♡ ♡

TODAY'S SUCSESS

WEATHER AND TEMPERATURE

WISH FOR TOMORROW

TODAY I'M GRATEFUL FOR . . .

DISTANCE SO FAR

STILL TO GO

ROOM FOR THOUGHTS, SKETCHES, PICTURES OR NOTES

STAGE

START LOCATION

DESTINATION

DATE

START TIME

DISTANCE

ARRIVAL TIME

ACCOMMODATION

I WILL REMEMBER THE DAY FOR . . .

MOOD

EFFORT

FLUID INTAKE

FOOT-HEALTH

BACKPACK-WEIGHT

STAGE - ATTRACTIVENESS

TODAY'S SUCSESS

WEATHER AND TEMPERATURE

WISH FOR TOMORROW

TODAY I'M GRATEFUL FOR . . .

DISTANCE SO FAR

STILL TO GO

ROOM FOR THOUGHTS, SKETCHES, PICTURES OR NOTES

SUMMARY

MY RECORDS

BIGGEST DISTANCE IN ONE DAY

EARLIEST START - TIME

HIGHEST MOUNTAIN

MY FAVOURITES

BEST VIEW

BEST SECTION OF THE TRAIL

SPECIAL ENCOUNTERS

WEATHER

TEMPERATURE

MOOD

EFFORT

FLUID INTAKE

FOOT - HEALTH

LANDSCAPE

TRAIL CONDITIONS

OVERALL RATING

BEST ACCOMMODATION

I WILL REMEMBER THE HIKE FOR . . .

1.

2.

3.

IN WHAT WAY DID THE HIKE DEVIATE FROM MY EXPECATIONS?

WHERE I SLEPT

○ COWBOY CAMPING   ○ HOSTEL
○ TARP ETC.   ○ HOTEL
○ TENT/HAMMOCK/ETC.   ○ FRIENDS
○ CAMPSITE   ○ TRAIL - ANGELS
○ SHELTER   ○ STRANGERS
○ HUT/BOTHY   ○ _____

MY BIGGEST CHALLENGES AND LESSONS

NOTES

IT'S NOT THE MOUNTAIN WE CONQUER, BUT OURSELVES.
EDMUND HILLARY

NOTES

SOME BEAUTIFUL PATHS CAN'T BE DISCOVERED WITHOUT GETTING LOST.
EROL OZAN

NOTES

THE WORLD REVEALS ITSELF TO THOSE WHO TRAVEL ON FOOT.
WERNER HERZOG

NOTES

IF WE CANNOT FIND A WAY, WE WILL MAKE ONE.
HANNIBAL

NOTES

SOMEWHERE BETWEEN THE START OF THE TRAIL AND THE END
IS THE MYSTERY WHY WE CHOOSE TO WALK.

UNKNOWN

Made in the USA
Monee, IL
22 May 2022